What people are saying.

**Poet Tree, an Anthology of Short Stories and Poems by Kathryn Cain and Steven Cain, featuring,
JD Widgery**

"What a wonderful collection of unique, fascinating short stories. All different, all remarkable, and all with a unique twist at the end. Hard to put down. From tales of farm life to Syfy, all rolled into a package of compelling pieces that quickly carries the reader from one to the next."
Greg Lamp, St. Paul, Minnesota

"Wow, your stories are wildly imaginative and really get you thinking in the abstract. Melissa describes them as "brief, poignant, and fantastical. They cause you to ponder reality and sometimes feel as if a dream has come to life. They are very entertaining and nicely sized morsels of fiction. I would read one or two at a time as a brief distraction during my work day".
Ted and Melissa Maillett, Vienna, Virginia

This Is The Truth

And All Its Lies

A Selection of Poems by

J. D. Widgery

**UPON THE
MOMENT**
PUBLISHING

TM

Upon The Moment Publishing, LLC

 ™

Books by Upon The Moment Publishing, LLC

From Novelist Kathryn Cain

    The Prophecy, Copyright © 2021

    The Uniting of Harverness, Copyright© 2021

    Simon Hunter, Copyright© 2022

    The Wolf, A Daniel Wolfgang Frasier Adventure, Copyright© 2023

    The House on Poland Hill, Copyright© 2024

From Novelist Steven Cain

    Sunset Kings, Copyright© 2020

    The Accident in Larson, Copyright © 2021

    War At Home, Copyright© 2022

    Bets & Breakfasts, Copyright© 2023

    Criminal Liaisons, Copyright© 2024

From the minds of Kathryn Cain, Steven Cain, and JD Widgery

    Poet Tree, An Anthology of Short Stories and Poems, Copyright©2024

Note: If you purchased this book without a cover, you should be aware that this book is stolen property. It was reported as "unsold and destroyed" to the publisher, and neither the author nor the publisher received any payment for this "stripped" book. Does not pertain to e-books.

This is a work of fiction. Any references to historical events, real people, establishments, organizations, or locales are intended only to provide a sense of authenticity and are used fictitiously. All the characters, names, organizations, and events are products of the author's imagination, and any resemblance to actual events, places, or persons, living or dead, is entirely coincidental.

This Is The Truth And All Its Lies, Copyright © 2024 by

Upon the Moment Publishing, LLC and Kathryn Cain, Revised January 2026

All rights reserved, including the right to reproduce this book or portions

thereof in any form whatsoever. For more information, e-mail

Uponthemoment@gmail.com, www.Kathryncain.com

Cover Design by Jasmine Widgery, Cover Illustration by Tracy Leung

Library of Congress Control Number: 2025913690

ISBN 979-8-9924876-3-3   Paperback $9.00

ISBN 979-8-9924876-4-0   E-Book $3.99

I dedicate this collection of poetry from the mind of and on behalf of my son, Jason David Widgery, to his beloved daughter, Jasmine K. Widgery. Jason passed away on March 30, 2024—a cherished, loving man who died way too soon. He saw our anthology come to life, The Poet Tree, before he passed into his new life. It includes works of his own. This collection, his story of love, perhaps, is taken from the written order in his notebooks. Some are titled. Some are not. I have numbered them for reference, but he asked that I keep them in their written form. So to you, my dear Jasmine, as promised, this publication of your Dad's work is for you.

All my love, Grandma.
Kathryn Cain

This Is The Truth

And All Its Lies

A Selection of Poems by

J. D. Widgery

Circa 1995 to 2024

J.D. Widgery

February 1995

Age 17

1

My Electricity went out
It's cold and dark
I just finished talking
To my love on the phone
She is leaving

I light up a cigarette
And cry
What will I do
How will I live
Why is she leaving
When will I see her again

Nothing
I won't
No one knows
Never

This Is The Truth
And All Its Lies

2

decisions

the things we do

can hurt

the things

we do

could be grand

Your grandfather
has a passion for life
he likes to see life
fulfilled, please, just
listen
to him...

the choice

is yours

I see a man who cares greatly for the young woman
I see a young woman losing face
I had the same conversation with my foster parents

Do what he says
He's a caring person
He reminds me of me...

Don't leave him
He needs someone
To take care of...
As do I

J.D. Widgery

3

From the dawn

      til the dusk

      from earth

      to Ocean

      Where rivers flow

      to where Dove soars

      Love and hate

      Pain and freedom

      to die

      to die

      to die

      in time

      in time

      The Pain

This Is The Truth
And All Its Lies

4

bow your head, my love

and hide your tears

Rest thy brow upon my breast

Never again live in fear

L
VE

        2
        Me
1   Love
Me   So
Love   True
So
Dear

        4
        Me
3   Love
Me   For
Love Two
So
Gone

...Our hearts may be Split in two

But they are still one...

J.D. Widgery

5

I tell myself not to cry
 on days gone so gloomy
tears, suffering from tombing
Why, Just Why

This Is The Truth
And All Its Lies

6

The untold boundaries

The tessera

The Mundane

The nothingness

The boundaries of those

untold tessera

so Your eyes

Are to Never

Be known

The Most non-mundane

Emotions are lost in the

Nothingness

There is No Way to tell You how much I Love You. There are the days in which we remember all too well, and all those days gone by. Those tears we've shared together and those all too alone. I know what I want. I know what I want to give. If I tried, I would break down, for I am not broken.

Our souls would Fill each other so deeply that Nothing in the world would bring us down. Life has kicked our ass. We Need to re-embrace each other with the warmth and the trust we had to even begin again. I am here For Your heart and Your mind. Let it go.

I ask these things. Let me in, Just a little at a time if need be. Just Please…Don't cry for what was lost; instead, reach out to Find it.
I give my life to you. You are the one I Love.
Just give me a chance to prove my worth to you.
I Love you, I Love You, I just want to hold you for Now.

Sorry, I didn't get time to Finish.
I'm in a hurry to come hold You.

Love Always and forever.

Jason

D.

Widgery

This Is The Truth
And All Its Lies

8

Daybreak has passed, settling upon eve, as my mind wondering upon my chores.
I Yearn Ya for another Kiss. Those lips that have been torn away too oft.
The rose in which thorn so tight, Your touch whose gentle awake brings dreams to the day.
Missing the subtle glance which Your provocative eyes peer into mine, tears wept in Silence
My Love for You goes uncharted; my heart knows no distance
My lips speak only of Your softness, and I die For Yours to touch

J.D. Widgery

9

What else is

there to tell

Over and over
I say her
Name crying tears
Of And Pain
A love lost
For more than
Years with nothing
Else to gain
But to suffer

the rose

Withered
   Dieing
Dead

   Crying
Pain
   End

beauty
   over
hunched

   Pricks
that
   bleed

My
   heart
too

Died

19
the bracelet

red, the red, red
rose it looked
as did I

From the love
I once remembered
Never again, lost

Elmo
She Named her
with passion
and laughter

25 cents
she drank
from the
glass I
gave her
a quarter
She threw
in was
mine It
Is again

This Is The Truth
And All Its Lies

9 continued

<u>the picture</u>

<u>Candy</u>

listen soFtly
MY dear

As quiet as You are
I know You can't hear

But when I speak,
   You listen

Lasting long
In my mind

Never speaking back
 Lost in Motion

    tired
    alone
    crying

I gave her
Heart-shaped
sweets
which she loves so
 Dearly
She left them
symbolizing something

HER NAME
    a picture
should never
be this grand

J.D. Widgery

10

I know I haven't written in a while...
It's just that I've nothing more to say
When I saw you the other day

11

I love being alone
Alone is having nothing
To live or die for
Alone has nothing
To fear
No pain to run from
No surprise for death

I love being alone
To hide from nothing
But myself
I know myself better
Than anyone
No one left to laugh
at me, but none

This Is The Truth
And All Its Lies

12

as the Night Farthens
The moon cries its tears
For the last

In the morning dew

as the sun Foretells
the glory and beauty
of the New Day

His opposition slowly
dies

13

Napkin doodle

It seemed all too sudden that the
Dawn Now arose. The hill was steep, Yet
All too easy. A tear Fell From the cheek
of the departed soul. Was life indeed narrow
but blind?

14

The forlorn pestilence of mankind
Bring Not only the life of the once
Forgotten, but the lies that come From it

15

Why die with a hand full of souls when you can die with two

16

As I look into her eyes, I witness her true passion for life letting one of never known to cry out in pain

17

When I feel her tears of blood, pain, and death
I alone at night gazing upon the wondering stars
knowing only that I alone am lingering in her heart.

This Is The Truth
And All Its Lies

18

Temptation is hard to resist. Good comes from None
So, if you're reading this, You're one nosy S.O.B.

Take me home, my dear; don't leave me here
with tears of envy, take me home, my darling
I can hear Your love calling with every desire to see me
Take me home, Whoever You are, Wherever are You ever Near or Far
I can't help the painful bleeding

19

In time, things must end
   Those hopes and dreams
     Once pondered
    Are now gone
Give thanks
   For what you have
     It may be nothing
    But It's Yours

J.D. Widgery

20

Funny King

  A pacifier to ease my pain
  To love me when No one cares
  The taste, the drome, the Yearning
  Nothing quite like my cigarette
  To keep me warm inside

21

Lying on the floor
     gasping for air

Reaching out for
     A breaking point

Living a lie
     Nothing ever true

Chances are
   It's a one-night stand

22

"it is true." She said
"that loving You would be the end."
I laughed, I cried, I fucked her again.

This Is The Truth
And All Its Lies

23

Alone with the Naked Garbage Man (Why?)

Why??? Oh Why
are telling all these lies
   Oh, Why??? Oh, Why
Can't the truth be told
   Oh, Why (Why)
are You so afraid
sitting behind on an empty chair
living a lie is all You know
crying
fall to Your Knees
let all Your Pain
and Sympathy just runs away

Tell me the truth
No need to lie
Just answer me this
Why ask Why?

Why Oh. Why
Are You so alone
Oh, Why oh Why
Does it have to be this way
Oh Why (Why)
It'll be the same tomorrow
No one will ever care
For You Oh No
Dying
It'll happen so soon

All the Pain and
Sorrow
Will all be here
tomorrow
No reason for you to
hide
Behind all of Your lies
If no one cares now
No one will care then
Just run away with
the
Naked garbage man

24

    Why is it, it is said, that when a man cries
he is lesser of a man....

> For it was Noon on Sunday
> I saw her cry for the first time
> As I Lay awake at Night, I wonder
> I wonder if it was for me whom she cried for
> or for herself

25

    I tried to call, but I couldn't. I was thinking of myself. I didn't know if I could handle talking to you without seeing or holding.

26

> Oh, What I would do
> Just to have one night
> with you
>
> It wouldn't matter what we did
> anything would almost feel right
> something mundane and small is big

This Is The Truth
And All Its Lies

    27

You ask why I spend time
discussing what I don't understand
I do. Why should I care? I do
You want to be somebody
You want to do something
with your life
<u>Not like this</u>

    28

It was awhile ago
and I thought I would
be able to let it all go

I was wrong

    29

I Know You're Here

30

I knew what she was doing, even though she didn't. I did.

31

Life sucks, and my death would please all
No one would cry
I live to die

32

                                                            To Live in thine eyes
                                                            To Die in thy lap

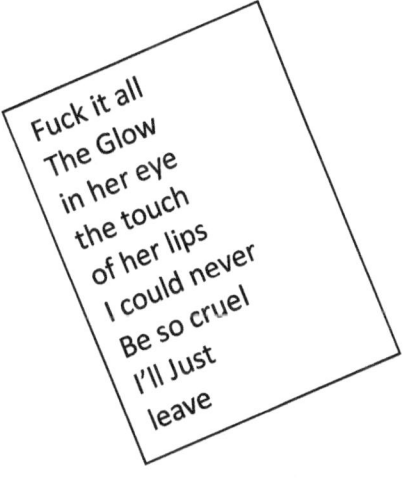

Fuck it all
The Glow
in her eye
the touch
of her lips
I could never
Be so cruel
I'll Just
leave

This Is The Truth
And All Its Lies

33

She may be lost
She may be out of bounds
all her tenderness and charm
maybe something a man like me
has never found
Her voice invites
Her eyes say more words
all trials and tribulations
there's nothing more assured
But in her woman's way
She's still a little girl
the things she wants
the things that she needs
oh well, the choice is hers
Because You can't take a woman
when she doesn't want you
and You can't be a man if You're
blind to reason

J.D. Widgery

34

Wholesome now
for the weak
Naked now
Only for the pure

Laying her upon my breast
Tear upon my cheek
Following a heart
That I once knew

Where am I
When to do
For my love
Was for another
Yet, I am in mourning
The pain is pleasant
For the misery is bearable
My wrongs have gone
No meaning
Only to find a joy
a bliss that was faced
and forgotten

This Is The Truth
And All Its Lies

35

I fell in love once
Once
then I stumbled out

36

I smiled today

For the first in so long

I wish I could only tell why

My thoughts are all more than one

My feelings are the same

Love is only once

Sometimes mistake

As a way out of

ones own life

bring only pain to

those all around

37

I am here now
Not of convenience
Nor in hiding
From what pain
I may have
I'm not here
because I know
You'll have me
I am here
because I love you
and I want my life back
all the things I want to say
all the sorrows I wish to give
are still not enough
I have nothing to offer
but my love
and I am sorry that it
may pain you so
I really don't know why I left
but I know that I was wrong
I made myself repress it all
to hold it all in and to
hide, in my own way
though it made everything worse
I'm glad you called that day
I can feel it now as I did
Only stronger because I've missed
You so long
If we can start a new life
together...

This Is The Truth
And All Its Lies

37 continued

have you seen me in the dark
Alone with my thoughts
have you known me to cry
without reason
have you tasted my tears
and then let go
to feel my smile
on your now damp
cheek
close your eyes
empty your thoughts
and feel
with your heart
don't cry
as I reach for
your hand
and hold you tight
For I know
all the loss
and all the gain
can never change
the way I feel
and the passion
in your eyes
make me even more...

J.D. Widgery

38

A fire and passion that once burned so bright
Flickered only to find a black flame
a truth that once was known was lost
only to appear a lie
When asked about those righteous days
I cry only knowing what was once held
so tight
I never thought
the cold, now to heart

39

it was only for a moment when I gazed upon her brow
she let me in
her eyes dark with a glowing

40

Welcome for when the sun sets
revealing the night sky
I know only that
In your eyes, will the
New days be bright

This Is The Truth
And All Its Lies
2007-2008
Ages 30-31

41

a lifetime of ignorance, fear, and pain
Naïve are we the stoup to the last
Levels of blissfulness
Artificial are we that stand
Valleys of endless dribble

42

I was in love once. You? Have you ever been in love?
I think so
Then you've never been. There is a selflessness
In love that can never be forgotten, a fire, a passion that
Fills your mind as much as your loins, a presence of emotion
depth shines in your eyes. A power essence that fills a void
known as your heart. All you do- is for love and not only
feel it but know it.

43

Ice in your eyes
An unbound truth
Never fleeing within

J.D. Widgery

44

Wisdom is an echo of thought, pondering existence.

45

    This morning, I awoke with a desire inside me
that couldn't bleed. For my love was gone.
    I forget such things from time to time.
for the thought drains my soul
    and I live no more
I no longer find love in all things
    Beauty in life is gone.

Tears fallen, lost in the rain
    sounds of the city, temper me

Running, going nowhere
    stuck in a life
    born of misery
    planted in death

Forgiveness is only a word
    to replace love
      in uselessness

This Is The Truth
And All Its Lies

46

Reality never Fails.
    Shattered dreams will come.

Nothing Matters
You do   to live
No place to call home

What happened
    No one knows

    Sorrow is the beginning and the end of suffering
Suffering makes us who we are
    As life changes us, who we were is gone
Stripped away by the pain.
    Pain is the result of life
        Life is pain
   out of control

47

Darkness falls
    blood
        screaming

48

above an ancient room
        inside a ruin
there is a jar
        where my heart lies

a canopic jar, No
        one of modern
hidden away
        by a dark soul

49

Each day, the wind blows
Softly, gently brushing your cheek
Whispering all unto your brow

Subtle then dangerous
Stripping the blind eye

50

Of all the beauty in the universe
Your smile was all I cared to know
Now I see the pestilence in your eyes
tears are lying

This Is The Truth
And All Its Lies

    50 continued

Children weep for the affection of their mother
Babies cry themselves to sleep in a flicker of darkness

Passion loving you, fear drives me

Life was a beautiful dream
   Now I am awake

I'm not scared anymore
   my dream is over
to be alone is a fate
I can no longer ignore

J.D. Widgery

51

Consciousness forbade my existence
swallowed by the shallow depths of sorrow

alone I weep
    still
    silent

Whispering
    why
    Nothing

Every man
    one man
No man

Sleeping
    more
No

52

If riches bring fortune
and fortune brings dreams
where do dreams without fortune bring you?

This Is The Truth
And All Its Lies

53

When children come into this world
    they cause pain
When children live their own lies
    they cause pain
When children leave this world
    they cause pain

There is only but a small moment
    where our children bring us joy
    take those moments
        keep them, hold on to them

    They are needed the most

54

Frozen Pizza, Hot dogs
Canned veggies, Mac N Cheese
        From a box
            Spam
Is that all that humanity
        has come to be?

55

It is Full again
    Life prepares itself
  love is lost
      aching

Alluring once was all
     Empty the places loved

Existence follows naked trails
   Flames now cold

56

I'll catch your midnight tears
Forever
I'll take all the pain
and burn it in the ocean
Fly away with all the sadness
hold you 'til the end of time

Free you of all things done
Lift the fear and kick its ass
Loving you is all I'll do
Follow me with all you have
And take me in
Your arms

This Is The Truth
And All Its Lies

57

Holding you now is only
   but a dream

58

I am a writer of words
   with no song
No strings to sing
   how I feel
No one to play
   My love
For existence and
   Scream my pain
     Away

J.D. Widgery

59

Constantly, I dream of nothing particular
   Seamless visions of pain
Flashes of pleasure and aching fear
   Rambling thoughts consume me

No importance in my life
   I follow nothing
     For my lethargy is my sin

I have become nothing
   For I have done nothing
Nothing I have
   She has all I love

The loss of my children
   Burns my soul
Confusion

I remember when dreams were remembered
   Not lost, but driven

This Is The Truth
And All Its Lies

60

Where do the children go
Where do they belong
Where should they be
Who should they be

61

We have lost ourselves
   Within ourselves
We have become what we want
   not what we want to be
We used to richly dream
   now, only dream of riches
We wanted so much for our children
   now our children miss us so much
We used to follow our hearts
   Tho the heart knows no soothe

62

Beauty in life is gone
  Happiness is missing
    Passion has died

63

Simply stained swallowed sin
    devoured by lies
I am no longer who I was
    I am no longer who I am
I am what I am; I am not
    what I am not
    I am not what I am

Sorrow sears sacred sin
    I know not who I am
I have forgotten all I know
    Forgotten all I am
Who am I

Sitting sadly sinning son
    Tears roll from cheek
Head always hanging low
    I am broken
To find not more
    Useless am I
For that, I have forgotten

This Is The Truth
And All Its Lies

64

Granted, I have seen many sorrows.
 Many pained. Children's tears draw me near as
they push me away. Dismay, Fear, and death. Pools
of blood and sand. An old woman weeps for her son. Dying to
protect his. Daughter jumps at the soldier,
angry cries fill the air.
 Another soldier tucked behind a fallen <u>vile</u> wall.
A shot in the amber dusk and the daughter falls. As does
the soldier she attacked for a <u>??? (unknown word)</u> is not shiv
proof.
A lieutenant draws enemy fire east into the city. Four follow.
The hidden soldier reveals his position as he retreats to
the fallen.
 "I am sorry, Bobby, I was too late," as he pulls
him into a broken building.
 Marines pour into the city. Shots are fired. A bomb
in an old striped Chevy. Six fall. Bobby shivers.
 "Happy birthday, buddy," the unknown soldier said.
Bobby laughs, "Fuken Funny asshole," his last words.
 Words the unknown soldier once hidden
will always remember. That soldier is now home.

65

Stupidity lies in all. Not kindness
 the irony of life brings us down
Patience is never found, only ignorance
 grant the children the lives of their own

66

People give only so they will receive
    they take all for themselves
Selfish are we all, in our own way
    Many needs we have, may we are
We are what we think we need
    to take care of ourselves first
Overinterpreted to suit our selfishness

67

I am finally alone
    Alone am I
Nothing but my thoughts
    keep mine company
I speak only to myself
    see none, but mine own
To sleep in a bed
    only for one
Is less painfully devouring
    than no children's laughter
to keep me awake
    I can not sleep

This Is The Truth
And All Its Lies

68

As I wander through it all
I do in wonder
I know nothing
My wisdom is false
My fear consumes me
I will miss all
that my life was
I have no rational thought
Logic has failed me
Truth is no longer valid

69

What happened to the happy Faces
 Where did the tears from love go
   the laughter is gone
A Father weeps, A mother laughs
   children lost
 daughters confused
   who do they love
where does their loyalty lie
   and still, the smile
 For they love all

J.D. Widgery

    70

Envision me
    as I was
the truth
 in my eyes
Is all
  I have left

    71

Take me home
   For mine is empty
Too quiet for my comfort
   A fire is my warmth
Nobody to keep me sane

This Is The Truth
And All Its Lies

72

Janice's Bike Ride
Janice is Five
   She loves the leaves in the trees
the flowers and the bees
   And happiness and laughter
make her feel alive

Never once has she cried
   laughter was all she knew
Swinging and playing
   And imagining that she Flew

Daddy bought her a bike
   a little big for her size
But she knew she could ride
   and many times, she tried

For days and days
   Daddy by her side
She tried, and she tried
on day five alone, she did ride
   and shortly, she Fell

Janice cried, and she cried
   even with Daddy at her side
He led her so tight
   and told her
of course, it will be alright
because you tried, and you tried
keep trying, and soon you will ride

J.D. Widgery

72 continued

With a kiss on her cheek
    He put her down by his side
Janice picked up her bike
    And began to ride

By herself, she would ride
    laughter and smiles
No one by her side
    Janice could fly

Look out your window
    She might be there
Flying on her bike
    To tears to be found
just wind in her hair

This Is The Truth
And All Its Lies

73

Janice Goes Fishing

Janice is Five
    Happy as can be
Sitting by the river
    watching the birds Fly low
And the fishy's she can see

She takes Daddy's hand
    and they walk to the bridge
and he gives her a box
    a fishing pole with a pink worm on the end

"Fishing's for boys, Daddy, you silly goose,"
    she says with a smile
"Fishing's for fun whoever you are," daddy replies
    with a tickle and a laugh
"Fishy's are smelly and slimy and Yuck."
    "Learn how to cast, and you'll love this stuff.
Casting is throwing the worm in the air."

She smiled and chuckled.
    And laughed a bit
"If I catch one, you're getting it."

She learned how to cast
    With the worm in the air
After a while, she caught one
    Finally, at last

J.D. Widgery

73 continued

She pulled on that pole
   And she fought that fish
hooked on the line
   "maybe it's a big one."
Daddy winked, and he grinned
   "Oh, Daddy, I wish!"

She reeled, and she reeled
   and she tried, and she tried
Daddy smiled before she cried
   "It's okay, honey; I am by your side."

Together, they pulled and reeled it in
   And soon, they discovered
with sweat on her head,
   "That's not a fish, Daddy!"
It was a boot instead

This Is The Truth
And All Its Lies

74

My thoughts are misgiven
   I cannot eat
      Not that I am sad
My jaw hurts

75

A man sits in a diner
   Many hours, days, it seems
Awaiting to see his children
   It is far from thee

76

Intrepid eyes consume
   wilted heart glows
only to envelope thy tears

77

To smile at you
   takes only a moment
but the emotion ensued
   Is eternal

78

Life. Perpetual despair
   Silenced only by the
Pain that ensues

79

Lost in your embrace
Your scent still haunts me
broken still
many years have passed
and my mind finds no peace
tranquil thoughts are no more

the earth, once shaken
by your presence
now molded into a deep well
ending nowhere
only to swallow my being
broken still

anger ensues me
as you display
and I always hide

You express
I feel
And you are gone

This Is The Truth
And All Its Lies

80

Love without expression
   Loses all meaning

Expression without love
   is a lie

Lost are we who love
   with lies

Embraced are we
   who lay with the
   one we love

81

Even apart, we are family
   Still in need of each other
     Selfish am I Not with my love
       For my children need all I have
        and more than I am able to offer
         the love of a mother, I am just a Father
       giving only a Father's love to the best possible
      children also need each other to share and hope
    together, they make it through the hard times
giving each other strength with the love of a
   Mother and a Father
     and of those who love them
       Family should be
     Always

J.D. Widgery

82

Grasping for life
   Still closed from the world
Nowhere I am led
   Only into the darkness
You have left me
   I fear to escape
For that is all I know

83

The best way to help yourself,
   Is to help others....
Believe it or not

   Late September was the end. October brought nothing but fear, pain, and loneliness. November begot hopelessness. December, a void into darkness and no theater to play.
   Everything serves purpose, good or bad. You may not have one without the other. Crock of shit, ain't it? You either do or you don't. Shitty thing is... so do other people, and you're stuck. Lost and hopeless...for god knows how long. And eventually, days, months, years, you move one. Placing whatever the hell it was that shit on you far back in your mind. Leaving only current thoughts to hide from.
   No one's life is perfect, no mind the media, people just...Suck. Me, You, Your lover...whatever...we are all selfish as a rule.

This Is The Truth
And All Its Lies

83 continued

"Survival of the Fittest." (1) Cliché, I know, but true and shitty. People with money donating to charities sounds nice and sweet and shit. Sure, it helps people in need, but they do it to feel better about themselves. Helping people makes you feel good, true, but so does masxxxxxxxxx. Both selfish. (but who brags about masxxxxxxxxx?)

A huge majority of the human population doesn't choose to have children (we all know how it happens.) And those who do don't even think about all the hardships and heartaches the child will go through in life. Having a child is the most perfect emotional high a parent can have. A person only chooses to have a child to make themselves feel good or better about themselves for many different reasons. Adopt if you can and help a child.

I love my children. One, my own, and one step...I would love nothing more than to be with them all the time. Teaching them, loving them, and watching them succeed in life much farther than anyone could dream. But their mother needs them, too. And they need their mother. It would be selfish of me to take them from her should the divorce go to court.

I cannot be selfish, especially with those I love. When I am in need, from companionship to enemies, it makes no difference. Those that I don't know or never met, I cannot deny my own selfishness...Have you ever walked by a Santa, ringing a bell, with a donation bucket, and said to yourself, "I would love to, but I can't afford it?" So you walk on by, well screw it, do it anyway.

Sit down and re-evaluate our life. It's interesting just to think and realize what life has to offer. Things come into place, and you can reconcile everything. Forgive all, including yourself.

Life is pain. Pain is life. Mourn and move on.

(1) Popularized by Herbert Spence and later used by Darwin.

J.D. Widgery

84

taunting are our thoughts
    confusion tears our mind
lifting logic
    emotion consumes
leaving only emptiness
    tears fall
with a still heart

85

leftovers sit
    still to the naked eye
as creatures breed and consume
    for that is all they know
growing only to lose their home
    living free until the end
time will pass
    left captive by their environment
Virus now to consume
    What is left
using all to adapt
    To what remains
the remains of their world
    Dwindle and rot
leaving man to suffer
    Into nothing

This Is The Truth
And All Its Lies

86

Captivating was she
   Stunning in a word
     of beauty
All things distorted
   Perfection in the way

87

Remember all things
   Past and present
Deny nothing lost and gained
   Pain and Joy
Accept life as it has become
   Bring Faith new
And become what life may bring
   Follow your heart
     Be yourself
      and thrive
   For the beauty of life

88

I followed a dream once
a dream I never dreamt
Passion to Follow
I never saw coming

Desire

I lost myself once
thinking I knew
what I wanted

89

Remember when I died
Remember when I lost
Remember when I cried
Remember when I
    Became

This Is The Truth
And All Its Lies

    90

Capture and motionless
My mind chants Forgiveness
Not for myself, For my love

I can forgive; I do forgive
Though pained...still
I Forgive because I
      Love

    91

I feel horrible, tired, and so fucking weak
I am so hungry. I feel as if I am to vomit
Sickness, I am afraid, has taken over
My years of coffee and cigarettes survival
Has finally caught up with me
I fear my daughter will not remember me
in years to come. Especially if my death is near

    92

a new life to come
   none a part of me
never warned
   sullen to abysmal pain

J.D. Widgery

93

Pray for me
    For I am Forsaken
Take me with you
    For I am lost
Hold me close
    For I am afraid

94

It's 2 am
I lay here, silent eyes open wide
the tic-tock of the clock
makes my empty home
even that more lonely

a train passes
reminding me of my youth
and how the El trains
used to calm me
and help me sleep

too long out of the city
in a desert of corn
a fan was enough to help
me sleep

This Is The Truth
And All Its Lies

    94 continued

Now nothing helps
Save extreme exhaustion
I fear my life is not
at a turning point
but a dismal end

tic toc
it is 4 am
I close my eyes
only because that bored

    95

What is consciousness: but knowing what the subconscious is doing?

    96

  I dance along the oaked trees
Whispering wind calls your name
  I crumble at the thought of what remains
Feeding off the fear that

J.D. Widgery

97

the art of dysfunction
never broken by the winds of trade

98

Options left over from choices made
Leave only imprisonment to more choices

99

I cry...I cry...I cry
not for the sorry or the pain
nor thy pleasure, and you
I just cry...
The reason, unknown to me
I don't know why
I cry...
something inside me
not as empty as I believed
open and finally naked
I am what I cry
finally myself, to me
I don't know why
though I cry

This Is The Truth
And All Its Lies

100

I can't let go
I can't
I feel more than I knew

101

Pain
    Stumbling ogres in my brain
    at war in my head
    pounding behind my eyes
    seizing the echoes of death

102

Combining my soul with the void of my heart
Absent of life, I know you felt
Naked to the source of all Her love
Never tainted by the negative forces or natural disasters
Fear my nothing
Nothing to lose
A man with nothing is to be feared, for he has nothing
Then there is love, love – from the French word for "egg"
– by thinking women can not find "love"
But they can feel more than man

J.D. Widgery
The after years

103

...Come Let Us Kiss and Part

I cried tonight
My love was lost
She always was

I've longed to be with her
But there's nothing I could do
If anything could go wrong
It was her
She knows but never acknowledged

As they say
"I feel lost..."

The last time we were together
I wanted to tell her
But I couldn't

I cry again
And leave her alone...
As she has left me

This Is The Truth
And All Its Lies

104

A vision of beauty...
The most memorable light in existence
Her brightness shone through the horizon
The day more enlightening than ever before
In the blink of an eye, she was gone
Fading setting back
Within the sorrowful darkness of life

105

She asked to talk to me
   Why do I feel this way
She sees me, I cry...
     Alone
       In love

Words mean nothing
   Thoughts and feelings
     Are everything

106

Acting is a big part of my life
   People say I'm good

They're wrong
   I'm hiding

I'm
sulking
now

why

just
to
see
her

is
to
feel
her

to
know
her

is
to
see

feeling
is
a
lie

This Is The Truth
And All Its Lies

108

I see you standing
At night
And still only see
Your shadow

Bothered, Yes, but not
By your
presence, rather, by your
assailing mood

J.D. Widgery

109

YOURS to MINE

Those eyes
full of light, hope, and dreams
stared upon me with grace
those sinful lips
that
cast their spell on me
oh...I still taste her
sweetness
those arms that held me
Upon thy breast
is yet still warm
thought this happy one
has never been
those eyes never
gazed on me
those lips
never touched
mine
those arms
held me not
that heart
never felt
I am no more
than I ever was
a being incapable of love
fears he feels for her
a shattered dream sifting away
through the hands of fate

This Is The Truth
And All Its Lies

110

Standing in the light, I feel the darkness
and the pain
in the darkness, I feel the light
with no pain

I take bad things and make them better
pain is no laughter
laughter is now more
not my pain

mine is hidden
under a shade of gray

agony enters my body
bursting
leaving only an irritated flame
if nothing at all

111

Why I am me helping others
and not myself
I know not

J.D. Widgery

112

Gazing up into the heavens cleanses my…
life of all impurities of
this sinful world
Me asking forgiveness, not deserving it
Standing alone, a "yes"

113

Wondering through the valley of my mind
    the vagabond reaches a standing point
one in which can never be defined
    the point of no return
a black hole preventing thoughts
    from continuing…
it's a ration of time, space, and the
constantly changing interlude
of existence

114

Something

                    Your life may seem worthless

You may not be able to walk down the street

                          Without being criticized

        You may be beaten, kicked, and spit upon

                          You may have nothing

But you at least you have a friend

            For with a friend is to truly have

everything

J.D. Widgery

115

   Oh, I love you so
More than anyone could know
     The past is no more

A true friendship lasts forever

From heart to the other, there is a smile

A smile is everlasting beauty

In your eyes, I see beauty and a lot of life

Happiness is beauty
    Beauty is life
      Life is happiness

This Is The Truth
And All Its Lies

116

I can't tell you how I feel
   I wish I could

I talk to you all the time
   and yet, I really don't

You say you don't understand
   but you really do

I don't understand why
   you act this way

In hiding...from your fears
   much like me

I can feel your true passion
   for life

I can feel your total sorrow
   It hurts

I can tell
   If you're in love

It too
   Hurts

When you're on the other side
   of the street

J.D. Widgery

116 continued

I know that you're hurt

Even when you smile

When you say to me
    how you are

I know it's not true
    Your lies are no good to me

You can't tell me
    that you don't care

Even a little bit
    shows through

As I look at you
    my heart is inflamed

There is more to you
    than body and soul

Tell me the truth
    no more lies

Something must be wrong
    or you wouldn't have to hide

I can tell you what you want
    I can give you what you need

Even if you won't even
    be with me

This Is The Truth
And All Its Lies

117

It feels like an axe
    buried into my skull

She doesn't love me
    like I do

I fall...
    She leaves me lay

she sleeps...
    I lift her up

I'd take her home
    she'd laugh at me

her heart
    it is true

mine
    is false

I am nothing
    she is everything

J.D. Widgery

118

I saw you last
   on a bleak winter's eve

with high intentions
   only to be pleased

I now feel
   that my needs were wrong

people who are so in love
   are the ones who are so strong

119

<u>Two Stand Alone</u>

  Alone...
  Waiting...
Love from one is not shared
 the other knows not what he needs
only what he wants...
 The beauty awaits feeling trapped
temptation has lured either of them
  against each other
They are no longer one

This Is The Truth
And All Its Lies

120

When I fall asleep at night
I see your provocative eyes
gazing upon mine

I feel your body
next to mine

I smell your hair

I kiss your lips

And you're not there

I hug my pillow
wishing it were you

But it's not the same

Oh, how I would love to
Be with you, then
And for all of eternity

No
A day is even too long

J.D. Widgery

121

What can I say
   I am no good with words

If beauty were sunshine…
   I would see you a billion miles away…

If the stars in the sky were your eyes…
   I would never stop looking…

If birdsong and the wind were your voice…
   I would always listen…

If the rain were your tears…
   I would catch them…

…and as the sun sets, the sky falls, the rain stops,
   And the birds and the wind die…

I still see you
   my heart is always here…

This Is The Truth
And All Its Lies

122

This is for you, my love

   In the past times we've had, they've all been bleak,
I've noticed a change in emotion. Although I know you're with another.
I know it's not true. Your love has left you; there's nothing you can do but sulk. As for me, I cry all the days and all the nights because I'm not with you the way I want to be, and there's nothing I can do.
   The feelings you give me are…enough to make the sun shine on a winter's twilight.

123

In
Your
Arms
Gently
Kiss
My
Cheek

124

Loathsome is he that fortifies his loss
Wrong is he who knows not why he is lost

J.D. Widgery

125

The pain once held so sacred
Now, only a long-forgotten desire
Belonging to no one
Aimlessly
Begot the threshold into fire
Passion once existed on in prayer
And lost within the soul of the undying

Death once bestowed to thee
Given away to the wrong
For the wrong
Lesser is he who knows not what is offered
Only taken

An eagle's past time
Blind above the sea

This Is The Truth
And All Its Lies

126

To live a lie is one of the only freedoms
Left to us from the beginning
Man has always desired to be
More than what he is worth
When women swoon
He should cry
Instead, he boasts

For the now
Only the now
Because of then

J.D. Widgery

127

Children playing in the snow
Are more than just angels
In the heavens
They are the peace within
All of us

It's too bad that the things
That we want
Just happen to be the things
We cannot have

A toddler smiles as her mother
Sweeps her off her feet
With a hug
Another weeps with love
For her sleeping todd

The good things change
And are followed by the bad
Not necessarily for the worst

The years have passed
Since a word been wrote
I have returned
In my grave
To lead my following self

This Is The Truth
And All Its Lies

128

First published in the anthology *Poet Tree,* published March 4, 2024

IN the END

Your eyes tell a man a lot of things
They tell more than happiness, sadness
Or anger
They say who you are

When I look into them, I hear your thoughts
I see your anger
I feel your pain
I taste the being in your being

I even smell your perfume
As you walk away

I don't know why I tell you how I feel
You only laugh, that beautiful laugh

That last kiss was nothing to you
To me, it was eternity

IN the End...
No one cares...

129

The darkness shatters through our hearts:
A friendship that will last forever.
Memories.
A fusion of love brings us together
Creating an eternal light for all to follow...

130

<u>Friends</u>

Friends are people who are there for you
They are people who know they can come to you
Why should we have friends
Without them, you have nothing, are nothing
For if you have everything but,
You still have nothing.

This Is The Truth
And All Its Lies

131

Someone loves her
No lie
Lip to lip
Cheek to cheek
And heart to heart
So true
I sit now and see her "love"
A depression tries
To break through
I hold back
I saw in her eyes
She truly cared
They closed
And lost all
In the beginning
The end was near
To see her laugh
I would cry
To see her smile
I would cry
She is happy
I am sad
She is in lust
I am in love
She is in love
I cry even more
I sit now with her
She feels of love
And grace
Now I leave

J.D. Widgery
132

as I walk along the rugged path of life
I gather upon a crossroads
I'm not too certain on how they are
All I know…is that its guidance
is narrow…yet far

I see aside me…a place
a tremendous sight…
land to roam free, in love and grace
the grass is green, the trees are tall
oh…how I wish I could join them…
…all

the birds coast among themselves
as the deer play in the meadow
the butterfly dances with elves
and the rabbits crouch and lay low

the sun shines bright, and the lilies
are more beautiful than ever before

I dance, and I sing, and I call your name
then I realize that you're never there
I sit on a rock under a willow on a hill
over the ocean, and I smile as a tear rolls
down my cheek

Now I know

as I sit on that rock
under that willow
on that hill
over that ocean

I stand
I fall
I die

This Is The Truth
And All Its Lies

133

You know there was a time when I believed
You know there was a time when I knew
You know there was a chance we'd be forever
And nothing would ever change between us

I lost myself and then couldn't find you
Oh, so scared, knowing not what to do
And I ran so far, far as my legs would carry
Following my shadow into the dark

Hiding from myself, hiding from you
Freeing myself from my fears
Locking up my insides
Never to be released

Changes brought on by pain entering
An exile of embarrassment and shame
Curling, twisting, and burning, knowing
Life would never be the same

Losing myself, I lost you more
Already lost to no end crying
I needed to reinvent myself
All that I gave, all that was given

Searching for a new hope
Seeking a new meaning in my life
Not knowing if the life I wanted
Was to ever be there again

J.D. Widgery

133 continued

I died so many years ago
Brought back by your love
Only to kill myself
I was so used to being alone

You know there was a time when I believed
You know there was a time when I knew
You know there was a chance we'd be forever

I lost myself in you
And I cried for so very long
All the faith in, I remember,
Knowing a love so true

Go with me
Though it will never
Be the same
Old endings for new beginnings

Just give me a second chance
Let me prove myself to you
I'll Never make the same mistake again
I want only to be true to you

We'll fly so far away
Just the three of us together
Just the three of us

This Is The Truth
And All Its Lies

134

Sitting in this corner
In the dark
Pondering existence
Wondering and boiling
And writhing and dying
And living and crying
And standing and laying
And lying.
The forces we see
At night
Are of those whom
We see in light
The pain we've served
The death we've deserved
Are all waiting

J.D. Widgery

135

First published in the anthology *Poet Tree,* published March 4, 2024

THE END
What am I doing here?
What purpose do I serve?
My life...It has no meaning?

Wondering through the wickedness of my
Mind
The devil finds my weakness
Raspingly, the phantom clogs my
Soul with this hatred

Trapped to see no end
Weapon in his hand
Blows his life away
(ending!!!)
Now condemned (so stay)

Alone in this wicked state
New life to begin
Disobey me once
You won't do so again

Questionable reference
Where'd you get this stuff?
That life has no truth
It's all shattered up.

Shot in the darkness, the victim falls

In light	I see darkness
In good	is evil
Hatred	love
In war	there is peace

This life of pure insanity

This Is The Truth
And All Its Lies

136

As I lay here in the darkness
I have found a place to hide
All alone, running from my fears
A passion that was never meant to be
She had ivory skin, sunflower hair
Eyes that spoke the softest words
And a voice that sang from the softest lips
I stand longing for death, and a tear rolls
from my cheek, she catches it
Why shed tears for something only a dream
Why shed the blood of thousands when
You can't even feel your own
Why dream a dream that can't be dreamt
Why the blood, tears, and pain
Why the torture ripping upon the words
And a love that was never there
As all the seas of life flowing into the
Oceans of love, bleeding into the rivers
The land grows as each man dies a death
All alone in fear from his own

J.D. Widgery

137

As each day passes
I truly never regret
For the love that
I feel
Is much stronger than
My loath, worry,
Or fear

As I sleep
As I sleep
You're with me
As much as I awake
Even when you're
Not even
Here

The passing
Dawns
Will bring a
New Year
One we will
Wed
And we're forever

Pure as spring
Rain
Are my dry tears
For your pain
Even though it doesn't
Show hurts me more
Thank you will ever know

In so many words
It has been told
In so many ways of
Old, but only one
Love of Love

This Is The Truth
And All Its Lies

138

Your beauty exceeds all greatness
When I see you, I'm back home
Sitting under my favorite willow
On my favorite hill overlooking the ocean
A twinkle in the sky, a bright reflection
Of your dancing beauty
Your smile
I feel an exertion of happiness and joy
Pulsating through my body
I rise up, soar through the horizon
And follow your eyes
To the dawn

J.D. Widgery
139

It was an early winter when we first met
Expected circumstances were not expected
Expressions of love were at first glance
Later in the eve, a slight turn of events
Had come sudden
My destination was not completed
Ignoring all long-found morals
My life had changed

Late spring, we ventured off
Learning things about each other
Which we never conceived of knowing
Our pastimes were of dancing in the rain
Watching sunsets and gazing at the stars

The next summer, it was all lost, though
Discovering others and not worrying
About what was to happen

A few years went by
And we'd forgotten each other
Until now

Now it's the same old thing
The rain, the dusk, the stars
Much more intense than remembered
But it all seems pointless

I learned to love her
And so could you
Remember your mother
As she will always be

This Is The Truth
And All Its Lies

140

There was a day when love grabbed ahold of each of us. Pulling
As an everlasting spring-drenching thirst. Creating
Giving life the joyful tears once deserved. Dreaming
 So close to make love, only the gentlest brush of hair. Wishing
Give no thought to what lay ahead, only feeling the now. Waiting
A kiss so soft and a tickle of an eyelash. Laughing

Pulling towards each heart, becoming one
Creating a flame not touched by darkness
Dreaming of a life to hold so true
Wishing, for a day never to part
Waiting for the next kiss
Laughing into the next day

Now, there is only fear and the pain, bringing anger. Pulling
The love seems hardly enough to hide what was lost. Creating
Tears of misery pour into the ocean, quenching no one. Dreaming
The slightest touch of hand brings swift turn. Wishing
Wondering the thoughts of the other alone in our own. Waiting
Even a kiss is twice thought with hidden eyes. Laughing

Pulling apart, lost in what should be
Creating more pain than what was
Dreaming of what will be
Wishing, for what once was
Waiting, time to heal what may not be
Laughing at the memory of once was

To love is certain
To live is also true
To live in love is quite possible
To live love successful is too

J.D. Widgery

140 continued

Remember the days all too well
Remember those days of love
Remember the passion
Remember it all

The happy and the sad
For the life you live is who you are
That cannot change
Don't love the memory
But the man you hold so true
Both lives have changed
Give love the chance to follow through

Give me a reason
Give me the faith
Give me the time
Give me a chance
A second is too late
Even a third
But a last

This Is The Truth
And All Its Lies

141

Of evening, once told
Lies unspoken
Tears lost in a dream
Fear of undying souls

Love fallen in days
Never seen
Burning slowly in
Depths of sin

This eve's only battle
Is those never known
Untouched lips and
Closed eyes

142

I've been waiting
Waiting for a time
A time that will never come

A precious moment
A moment with you
The time will never come

Hopes and dreams shattered
And lost without recognition

J.D. Widgery

143

An offering to the unwanted
An ode to the betrayal

The children of the world
Come together
To bring forth a smile
To the future

Never knowing the
Immortal words of love
Only their love of life
Bringing only joy and happiness
To each other

144

Nothing when I call you
Nothing when I sing
Nothing when I whisper
Nothing cause nothing stays the same

Remember when
Remember why

That day
When together
We walked
All alone
To the sea, we fell

This Is The Truth
And All Its Lies

145

The tears that follow the ultimate pain and suffering
Of the ever-more
The last days of a vacant home
Endless voices in my head
Experience the death at length
An ocean of blood, filled from tears
Sacrifice yourself to the one you love
Or yield your pastime
Accept your passion for what it was
Truth of what is will be
Never was
As your fear grows of what has been done
Your fear knows none the less of what has
To be done
Every morrow, I sing
Why in God's name do I envy you
We would have been so much together

J.D. Widgery

146

Alone in the darkness
Of this cold stone earth
The fire burns deep in
My charcoal heart
Profuse, blood-red hatred
Burst upon my boil
Leaving only rotting flesh
And bones and death

Feasting on still-warm brains
Gnawing on beating hearts
Spitting out veins stuck in my teeth
The pain and death
(wimpy man)

Tears on your pillow
Crying on your knees
Begging for Forgiveness

I laugh at thee...

This Is The Truth
And All Its Lies

147

It was a past time
Once forgotten
All that was lost
Now begins anew

Never shouting what was true
But what, only what was seen

Tomorrow, a new light will spawn
Tonight, we wait for dawn

148

Castaway on mine own
Given the time
All alone
Building a fire
For your touch
Longing for warmth

149

Kiss me oh tainted one
For I know not
What passions may lay ahead
Only in the now am I so certain
The past held so many tears
The new yet to be re-discovered

J.D. Widgery

150

Only a fool's heart may not cry for what is feared
Only a king's heart cries for what is true

151

Quick
Hold
Me
Before
I sleep
Slowly
Carry
Me

152

The right things said
The right things done
The best things that happen
The best things to come
The loving womb
The tender kiss
My hand on yours
Is not all I miss

This Is The Truth
And All Its Lies

153

Living a dream for the dream's sake
Never knowing the truth inside
Emotions so strong
The fire in your eyes isn't soothed by the blood
Giving hope to the lost souls
Enslaving those who are free
Battling those of peace
Bearing the weight of those
Burdens we all take for granted

154

Three seasons passed
A day only so long
Nothing can compare
Nothing else can matter
I dance
I sing
I cry
For your love
I've fallen for you
All too long ago

J.D. Widgery

155

First published in the anthology *Poet Tree,* published March 4, 2024

The Affair

It was a mid-afternoon in mid-May; in fact, it was a Sunday. A woman with explicit stature and prose happened upon me. I was quite impressed with her form upon approach and honestly shocked at how the following of events took (speaking of my actions). I will tell you the story, but first, I will explain myself.

I am a man early twenties, a good Christian man, and have never been subject to an action of unearthly pleasure. Engaged to be married in the later summer, yet still untouched by persuasion. I have been gone many months in school while my love lays at home wondering when I shall return. I write her and tell of the many nights I gaze upon the stars, knowing that those are the same stars she sees and wishing to see the day we gaze together... Arm in arm, reciting poems and dreaming of our children after we wed.

I am a poet by heart, and I attend one of the most respected schools in England...As I was saying.... This magnificent perfection of a woman, which whom I did notice in church early in the morning, ran into me yet again in the marketplace...

"When were these fruits picked," she so gently asked. Shocked that I looked so common, I almost abruptly responded in the rue, but I caught myself saying, "I'm sorry?" Stuttering, "I don't work here. I can't be much assistance."

"Oh, I do apologize." Pauses, "Yes, you were at service this morning. The choir did magnificently well."

"Well, thank you," almost as if I'd known her a lifetime. "We've worked so hard to become so."

Her eyes brighter than any star I had gazed upon, and a smile more enlightening than the heavens in the sky. Skin soft as doves and hands of such power and strength. Her voice soft and light,

This Is The Truth
And All Its Lies

155 continued

the German accent, sharp and poignant. I had never, ever thought such physical perfection could exist.

The conversation went on, though I didn't pay close attention, for I was engaged in other thinking...and soon found myself grasping her hand and walking along the creek as young lovers do in the springtime.

I soon discovered that we shared common interests, we shared the same passions, and had the same dreams. We sat under a willow aside the stream and made a picnic with our groceries. Laughing at each other's experiences and crying at our pains.

That last glass of champagne was the sweetest, for by then, it was Monday, the sun had risen, and we kissed upon its arrival. As the day had dawned and we grew closer, we walked on...

"I live just up this path...would you like to freshen?"

"Why, yes, I would, in fact I would, be so pleasantly honored to enter your abode..."

"A fine cup of tea then?"

"Yes."

A few days passed, and I had not yet finished my remembrance of an evening of elegance. Now, since the semester was at leave, and since I could not afford to get back home, I decided to rent a cottage home for the week.

My room was located on the west side of the house, where you can see the sun rise and set over a mountain top. Each night, I watched, dreaming of her unsurpassable beauty...

One eve, on my way to dine, I noticed a familiar smile. Yes it was she, just one room over, how pleasant it feels.

"Oh, hello, I've been wondering about you. Why haven't you come by? You remember where I live?"

"Why, yes, I remember. I was just afraid you didn't want to be just yet for of my commitment back home..."

"You must always follow your heart and soul...Always."

J.D. Widgery

155 continued

      Deep in my mind, I kept trying to think of why I couldn't be with her, even as much as I've wanted to. The woman I've loved for years? I couldn't remember what she looked like...Or even her name...I felt wrong; I did, though, see an old willow and rain flash in and out of my mind.
      It was a love affair. No one knew...or could ever find out. There had to be a reason for this opportunity. It was a test of a sort, a test of Faith, God's and Serina's...It's too sad I was about to fail. For this creature, of such compassion and love of life, was all I could think.
      We came together, as two deer would at a stream, soft and so full of the things in life that are worth living for.

End

www.ingramcontent.com/pod-product-compliance
Lightning Source LLC
Chambersburg PA
CBHW031407040426
42444CB00005B/454